I.   INTRODUCTION AND SUMMARY

With the aging of the baby boom generation, a growing number of our nation's investors are at or near retirement age. Indeed, data presented at the first *"Seniors Summit"* held by the Securities and Exchange Commission (SEC) in July 2006 indicated that 75% of the nation's consumer financial assets, valued at $16 trillion, are held by households headed by someone who is 50 or older. Within the next 20 years, 75 million people will have celebrated their 60th birthday. Because these "senior investors" are a growing segment of investors, financial services firms are increasingly focusing their marketing and sales of investment products towards the senior investor or those investors nearing retirement age. Within this broader context, securities regulators are concerned about the possibility of unscrupulous and abusive sales practices and investment frauds targeted towards senior investors. In fact, some data indicates that although individuals aged 60 or older make up 15% of the U.S. population, they account for 30% of fraud victims.[1]

In response to this concern, in May 2006, the SEC and the North American Securities Administrators Association (NASAA) announced a coordinated national initiative designed to protect seniors from investment fraud and sales of unsuitable securities.[2] Working together with the NASD and the NYSE Member Regulation Inc. (now consolidated as the Financial Industry Regulatory Authority, or FINRA), the SEC and NASAA initiative includes three components: active investor education and outreach to seniors and those nearing retirement age; targeted examinations to detect abusive sales tactics aimed at seniors; and aggressive enforcement of securities laws in cases of fraud against seniors. This joint and collaborative initiative by securities regulators is designed to build on the existing efforts that each regulator had underway, toward a shared mission to protect senior investors. This initiative is active and ongoing.

As part of this effort to protect senior investors, regulators initiated a series of coordinated on-site examinations of broker-dealers, investment advisers and other financial services firms that offer so-called "free lunch" sales seminars. These seminars are widely offered by financial services firms seeking to sell financial products, and they often include a free meal for attendees. Sales seminars are often advertised in local newspapers, through mass-mailed invitations, mass-email, and on websites. While specific data is not available regarding the actual number of sales seminars being conducted, regulators believe that the number of sales seminars has increased in recent years, as financial services firms are increasingly seeking to provide advice to seniors and those approaching retirement.

---

[1]   *"NASAA Survey Shows Senior Investment Fraud Accounts for Nearly Half of all Complaints Received by State Securities Regulators,"* (July 17, 2006), available at http://www.nasaa.org/NASAA_Newsroom/Current_NASAA_Headlines/4998.cfm.

[2]   *"Securities and Exchange Commission and North American Securities Administrators Association Launch Program to Protect Senior Investors,"* (May 8, 2006), joint SEC and NASAA press release available at http://www.sec.gov/news/press/2006/2006-65.htm.

Examinations were targeted in areas of the country that have large populations of retirees. Examinations were conducted in Florida, California, Texas, Arizona, North Carolina, Alabama and South Carolina by state securities regulators in those states, NASD and the NYSE Member Regulation Inc. (now FINRA) and the SEC. This report summarizes the results of these examinations and was prepared by the SEC's Office of Compliance Inspections and Examinations, NASAA and FINRA (collectively, referred to in this Report as regulators or examiners).[3]

The purpose of the examinations was to review firms that offer sales seminars targeted to seniors and retirees for compliance with securities laws and rules (federal, state and self-regulatory organization (SRO) rules) designed to protect investors. Specifically, the examinations reviewed:

- Advertisements, seminar materials, and sales literature for any misrepresentations, exaggerations, or omissions of material information;

- Customer transactions engendered by these seminars to evaluate the suitability of investment recommendations that were made; and

- Supervisory systems, policies, and procedures used to detect and prevent violations of the securities laws for adequacy.

We conducted 110 examinations between April 2006 and June 2007. While each of our findings is described in greater detail in this report, in sum, we found that:

- **Sponsors of "free lunch" sales seminars offer attractive inducements to attend**. The seminars are commonly held at upscale hotels, restaurants, retirement communities and golf courses. In addition to providing a free meal, the firms and individuals that conduct these seminars often use other incentives (*e.g.*, door prizes, free books, and vacation deals) to encourage attendance.

- **Often, the target attendees are seniors**. Many of the "free lunch" sales seminars are designed to solicit seniors. They are advertised with names like "*Seniors Financial Survival Seminar*" or "*Senior Financial Safety Workshop*," and offer "free" advice by "experts" on how to attain a secure retirement, or offer financial planning or inheritance advice. The advertisements used to solicit attendees often imply that there is an urgency to attend. For example, invitations include phrases such as "limited seating available" or "call *now* to reserve a seat." Some illustrative examples of advertisements used for sales seminars can be found in Appendix A to this report.

---

[3] This report includes examination findings of the SEC's staff, FINRA's staff and the staff of the individual states regulatory authorities, which are not findings or conclusions of the Securities and Exchange Commission, FINRA or NASAA. This report includes findings from examinations conducted by NASD and NYSE Regulation Inc, now FINRA.

- **Seminars are designed to sell.** Many sales seminars were advertised as "educational," "workshops," and "nothing will be sold at this workshop," and many advertisements did not mention any investment products. Nonetheless, the seminars were intended to result in the attendees' opening new accounts with the sponsoring firm and, ultimately, in the sales of investment products, if not at the seminar itself, then in follow-up contacts with the attendees. To the extent that participants may attend a seminar in order to obtain educational insights and information, they should be aware that the primary goal of the sponsors of these "free lunch" seminars is to obtain new customers and sell investment products. Examiners found that the most commonly discussed products at the sales seminars were variable annuities, real estate investment trusts, equity indexed annuities, mutual funds, private placements of speculative securities (such as oil and gas interests) and reverse mortgages.

- **Some firms had particular compliance and supervisory controls that appeared to be effective. And, during a small number of the examinations (5 examination or 4% of those conducted), regulators found no problems or deficiencies.** During examinations, regulators identified specific compliance and supervisory practices that appeared to be effective in ensuring compliance with the securities laws and rules. For example, one broker-dealer required its employees to forward all materials to its home office for a supervisory and compliance review prior to using the materials at sales seminars. Another broker-dealer utilized checklists to aid supervisors with the approval process for seminars and seminar materials. More detailed examples of these practices are set forth in Appendix B to this report.

- **Half of the examinations found that firms used advertising and sales materials that may have been misleading or exaggerated or included seemingly unwarranted claims (in 63 of 110 examinations, or 57%). Many broker-dealer firms did not submit their sales material to NASD (now FINRA) for review, as required by NASD advertising rules.** The most common types of apparently misleading statements appeared on mailers and advertisements for the sales seminars, and involved statements about the safety, liquidity or anticipated rates of return. Statements included, for example: "Immediately add $100,000 to your net worth," "How to receive a 13.3% return," and "How $100K can pay 1 Million Dollars to Your Heirs." Additionally, some sales materials made comparisons between dissimilar investments or services, included representations about the expertise or credentials of the registered representative that may have been misleading or confusing, or involved testimonials that may have been misleading.

- **Individuals attending the sales seminars may not understand that the seminar is sponsored by an undisclosed company with a financial interest in product sales.** The mailers and advertisements for the sales seminars often focused on the individuals who would be conducting the seminar, and often included the name of the registered representative or investment adviser, a photograph and information about his/her background as an expert in providing investment advice, and his/her history in the local community. Individuals who attend the seminars or who are considering attending are not always provided with the name of the firm sponsoring the seminar, and may not be aware that product sponsors (*e.g.*, mutual fund companies and insurance companies) may provide funding for the seminars with the expectation that investment professionals will sell their products. In these situations, seminar attendees may not have known that the financial adviser speaking at the seminar was not unbiased in making product recommendations.

- **Many examinations found indications that firms had poorly supervised these sales seminars.** Examiners found indications of weak supervisory practices in 65 of the 110 examinations (or 59% of the examinations conducted). For example, a common finding was that firms had inadequate supervisory procedures or had not implemented their procedures with respect to sales seminars held by their employees.

- **Some examinations found indications that registered representatives or investment advisers holding the sales seminars had recommended investments that did not appear to be suitable for the individual customers.** In 25 of the 110 examinations (or 23% of examinations conducted), examiners found indications that unsuitable recommendations to purchase investments were made at the sales seminars, or following the seminar when an attendee opened an account. The investments appeared to be unsuitable in light of the customers' investment objectives or time horizon – *e.g.*, a risky investment was recommended to an investor with a "conservative" investment objective, or an illiquid investment was recommended to an investor with a short-term need for cash.

- **In some instances, the sales seminars may have involved fraud.** Examiners found indications of possible fraudulent practices in 14 examinations (or 13% of the examinations conducted), that involved potentially serious misrepresentations of risk and return, liquidation of accounts without the customer's knowledge or consent, and sales of fictitious investments.

As a result of the examinations, most firms have received deficiency letters or letters of caution that outlined apparent rule violations and deficiencies and requested that the firms examined take corrective actions (these letters were provided to 86 firms, or 78% of all examinations conducted). In addition, some examinations (25 of the 110, or 23%) are under review for possible further investigation or action by a state, FINRA or SEC.[4]

The results of these examinations lead regulators to conclude that financial services firms should take steps to supervise sales seminars more closely, and specifically take steps to

---

[4] Many examinations had multiple dispositions. For example, a deficiency letter may have been provided to the firm requesting corrective action, and findings from that exam may also have been referred for possible disciplinary or enforcement action.

review and approve all advertisements and sales materials for accuracy. In addition, firms should redouble efforts to ensure that the investment recommendations they make to seniors are suitable in light of the particular customer's investment objectives.

Regulators have compiled a list of supervisory practices that have been identified during examinations and that appeared to be effective, which is included in Appendix B of this report. This information may assist firms in considering their own supervisory practices with respect to sales seminars. Regulators further urge financial services firms to take steps to assure that supervisory procedures with respect to sales seminars are being implemented effectively. Regulators participating in these examinations will continue to focus examination, enforcement and regulatory efforts on the use of sales seminars targeted to seniors.

In addition, regulators conclude that, because seniors are targeted as attendees for sales seminars, ongoing investor education efforts for seniors should provide education with respect to "free lunch" sales seminars. Specifically, senior investors should understand that these are *sales* seminars -- that is, they are intended to result in the sales of financial products, and they may be sponsored by an undisclosed company with a financial interest in product sales. Investor education efforts should emphasize that, despite the claims of urgency that are sometimes made by sponsors of sales seminars, and in light of the possibility of misleading or exaggerated statements or claims about investment products or the expertise of the financial adviser, investors should take time to research the firm, the financial adviser as well as the product being offered before opening an account or making a purchase. Regulators make a variety of tools available to investors to assist them in understanding investment products and investigating a broker or other financial professional before investing, and many of these tools are listed in Appendix C to this report.

II.   BACKGROUND: RISK ASSESSMENT AND SELECTION OF FIRMS FOR EXAMINATION

As a threshold matter, regulators focused on geographic areas with high populations of seniors. Thus, examinations were first initiated in Florida by the Florida Office of Financial Regulation, NASD and NYSE (now FINRA), and SEC staff. The examinations were then expanded to include other states in geographic areas that had large concentrations of senior citizens. Based on census data, some of the states with the highest senior populations were Florida, California and Texas, among others. In addition, census information reflected a high concentration of retirees in the states of Arizona, North Carolina, Alabama and South Carolina.[5] Regulators in each of these states and examiners from the NASD, the NYSE and the SEC commenced coordinated examinations during 2006 and 2007.

To identify firms for examination, regulators collected publicly available information including advertisements, invitations and websites that sought to target seniors for "free

---

[5]   U.S. Census Bureau, *Current Population Reports, 65+ in the United States* (Washington, D.C.: U.S. Government Printing Office, 2005), 23-209.

lunch" seminars. Examiners then developed a risk assessment model to identify the firms that appeared to present the highest risk of possible violations. Regulators considered the following factors in conducting this risk assessment:

- Whether the advertisements and/or sales literature appeared to target senior citizens;

- Whether the advertisements and/or sales literature appeared to have exaggerated, misleading and/or fraudulent representations, including testimonials;

- Whether the advertisements and/or sales literature discussed or referred to securities that appeared to be of high risk to the average senior citizen;

- Whether the entities/individuals identified in the advertisements and/or sales literature were appropriately registered to sell the securities discussed or referenced in the advertisements and/or sales literature;

- Whether the entities and/or individuals identified in the advertisements and/or sales literature had any prior disciplinary history and/or customer complaints within the last year;

- Whether the advertisements and/or sales literature, when used by a broker-dealer, were filed with and reviewed by NASD pursuant to NASD's advertising rules; and

- Whether the advertisements and/or sales literature offered any incentives to attend the seminars (*e.g.*, prizes, trips, or books).

The regulators then evaluated the risk assessment data and selected firms for examination. Frequent communication among the regulators helped to ensure a consistent approach to examinations, and prevented any duplication in examinations.

The NASD's Department of Advertising Regulation was an integral part of the examination process. For broker-dealer firms, all advertisements and seminar sales literature were reviewed by NASD personnel to determine if the literature was in compliance with NASD's advertising rules. NASD's staff then provided each regulator conducting the examination with information about any areas of apparent non-compliance.

Each regulator conducted examinations. Some examinations were conducted jointly by state regulators and the NYSE or the SEC. Examinations included interviews with firm employees and reviews of records maintained by the firm. In their examination process, state regulators attended some sales seminars to ascertain what was being said during seminar presentations. Regulators followed their own protocols for examination process and disposition. Upon completion, some examination findings were referred to the most appropriate regulatory authority to handle the matter based on the types of potential violations identified.

Most of the firms examined were registered as broker-dealers, and many were also registered as investment advisers with a state or with the SEC. Some firms were registered as investment advisers, but not as broker-dealers. Employees of the firms examined were often licensed as registered representatives with NASD, and may also have been advisory representatives with the state, or advisers registered with the SEC. A small number of firms were not required to be registered under state or federal securities laws, and were examined by state regulators. The firms examined ranged in size and type -- from independent contractors at small firms to large firms with branch offices across the country -- although most were small local or regional firms. Many examinations were conducted at branch offices.

III. KEY SECURITIES LAWS AND REGULATIONS APPLICABLE TO SALES SEMINARS[6]

Registration: Sales seminars may be conducted by a registered representative, investment adviser or an unregistered person. Absent any exception or exemption, any firm that sells securities (as defined by the Securities Exchange Act of 1934, *e.g.*, stocks, bonds) must be registered as a broker-dealer. In addition, in order to discuss securities at a seminar sponsored by a broker-dealer, the presenter must be a licensed registered representative (under NASD Rule IM-1031 and NYSE Rule 345[7]). Investment advisers provide investment advice to purchase or sell securities for compensation and as part of a regular business. Investment advisers also sponsor sales seminars, and they may be required to be registered either with a state or with the SEC. Many sales seminars are designed to sell non-securities products (*e.g.*, insurance). Only firms selling or advising the purchase or sale of securities products are required to be registered.

Sales Literature: The materials used or distributed by broker-dealers at seminars are considered "sales literature" and are subject to the supervisory approval and record-keeping requirements under NASD and NYSE rules. In addition, these rules apply to any communications that are used to promote the seminars, such as advertisements in print, on the web or by radio or television broadcast.[8] Under these rules, sales literature must be approved by a registered principal prior to the seminar; the firm must maintain all sales literature in a separate file for three years; and the file must include the name of the registered principal that approved the seminar and the materials distributed at the seminar

---

[6]   Individual states' securities laws also apply.

[7]   NASD and NYSE rules are separately cited in this report, as a common FINRA rulebook has not yet been developed.

[8]   Specifically, each advertisement, market letter, sales literature or other similar type of communication which is generally distributed or made available by a member firm to customers or to the public must be approved in advance by an allied member, supervisory analyst, or qualified person (under NYSE Rule 342(b)(1)).

(under NASD Rule 2210(b) and NYSE Rule 472(d)). The broker-dealer must also maintain information concerning the source of any illustrative data used in the seminar (under NASD Rule 2210(b)(2)(B)).

Seminars are public appearances, as are radio or television interviews or other speaking activities (under NASD Rule 2210 and NYSE Rule 472(1)). NASD and NYSE rules require that: "all member communications with the public shall be based on principles of fair dealing and good faith, must be fair and balanced, and must provide a sound basis for evaluating the facts in regard to any particular security or type of security, industry or service" (under NASD Rule 2210(d)(1)(A) and NYSE Rule 472(i)). These standards also apply to registered representatives' participation at seminars.

Anti-Fraud Rules: Federal and state securities laws and SRO rules prohibit making any untrue statement of a material fact, or omitting to state a material fact that is necessary to make the statements that are made not misleading (*e.g.,* under Section 17(a) of the Securities Act of 1934, Section 10(b) of the Exchange Act and Rule 10b-5, and Section 206 of the Investment Advisers Act of 1940).

Investment advisers (whether registered with the SEC or state or not) also have a fiduciary duty to provide full and fair disclosure of all material facts to their clients and their prospective clients. All advertising materials and other materials distributed at a seminar by an adviser are subject to these restrictions, including any representations about the adviser, its business and investment advice, such as performance data, investment strategies, education, background and experience (under Section 206 of the Advisers Act).

It is fraudulent for an SEC-registered adviser to distribute advertisements that contain or refer to testimonials or past specific recommendations that were profitable (under Rule 206(4)-1 under the Advisers Act). In addition, SEC-registered advisers cannot use advertisements that imply that a graph, chart, or formula will enable investors to make their own investment decisions without disclosing the limitations or difficulties of the approach (under Rule 206(4)-1 under the Advisers Act and various state securities statutes). Advisers may also not falsely promise to provide free services (Rule 206(4)-1 under the Advisers Act).

Broker-dealers may not make exaggerated or misleading endorsements of investments, and unwarranted predictions or projections of investment performance are also prohibited (under NASD Rules 2210(d)(1)(B), (d)(1)(d) and NYSE Rule 472(i)). In addition, broker-dealer testimonials must also include certain information: (1) the fact that the testimonial may not be representative of the experience of other customers; (2) the fact that the testimonial is not indicative of future performance or success; and (3) if more than a nominal sum is paid, the fact that it is a paid testimonial (under NASD Rule 2210(d)(2)(A) and NYSE Rule 472(j)(7)).

To prohibit potentially misleading advertisements and to ensure that communications are fair and balanced, NASD rules require that broker-dealers provide certain sales literature to its Department of Advertising Regulation for review. For example, advertisements and sales literature concerning mutual funds and variable annuities must be submitted to the FINRA for approval within 10 days of the time it is first used or published (under NASD Rule 2210(c)(2)(A)). Firms may also voluntarily submit other material for FINRA review and must pre-file other advertisements in some cases.

Duty to Recommend Securities that are Suitable: A broker-dealer may only recommend a security to a customer that it has determined is suitable for that customer in light of that customer's particular age, financial situation, risk tolerance, and investment objectives (*e.g.*, under NASD Rule 2310 and IM 2310-2 and NYSE Rule 405). Broker-dealers must obtain the customer's name, tax identification number, address, telephone number, date of birth, employment status, annual income, net worth, and investment objectives for each retail customer account (under Exchange Act Rule 17a-3(a)(17)(i)(A)). As a fiduciary, an adviser has an obligation to deal fairly with its clients and to act in their best interests (under Section 206 of the Advisers Act).

Supervisory Requirements: Broker-dealers must establish, maintain, and enforce written supervisory procedures to supervise the types of business in which they engage and to supervise the activities of registered representatives, registered principals, and other associated persons (under Section 15(b) of the Exchange Act and NASD Rule 3010(b) and NYSE Rule 342)). Similarly, investment advisers must adopt and implement written policies and procedures reasonably designed to prevent violations of the Advisers Act by the adviser or any of its supervised persons (Section 206 of the Investment Advisers Act and Rule 206(4)-7(a) thereunder).

IV.   EXAMINATION FINDINGS

- **Sponsors of "free lunch" sales seminars often offer attractive inducements to attend**.

We found that sales seminars are commonly held at upscale hotels, restaurants, retirement homes, golf courses and other locations. A few were held at the offices of the firm sponsoring the seminar. Invitees were from the local community. Generally, the seminars were free. In some cases, in addition to providing a free meal, the firms and individuals that conducted these seminars used other incentives such as door prizes, free books ("A Free Tax Payer Awareness Guide"), free portfolio reviews and one even offered a $250 discount on a nursing home protection planning session. To further encourage attendance, some advertisements offered seminar attendees eligibility to win prizes such as tote bags, gift certificates or even a 3 night/4 day cruise for two.

- **Often, the target attendees are seniors**.

We found that many of the seminars were designed to appeal specifically to seniors. Some seminars also targeted religious affinities or associated groups such as the military. Many sales seminars were advertised in local newspapers or attendees were solicited to attend via mass invitations sent through the mail or via email. Many solicitations targeted seniors. Samples of advertisements can be found in Appendix A to this report.

The seminars had titles such as: *"Senior Financial Survival Seminar," "Senior Citizen Tax Specialist," "Senior Financial Safety Workshop,"* and *"Senior Citizen Retirement and Asset Protection Education Workshop."* Some communications explicitly stated that attendance was limited to those between, *e.g.*, 60 and 85 years of age, or over 70 years of age. In the advertisements and/or invitations, the seminar sponsors often claim to offer advice on how to attain a secure retirement, financial planning, inheritance advice, and even "nursing home asset protection." Often, the ads and mailers featured photographs of happy and attractive seniors – perhaps to suggest that an attendee could achieve financial security or prosperity by attending the seminar.

Seminar sponsors appeared to target seniors, and to seek to limit attendance by the non-target attendees. Some ads and mailers were explicit in excluding attendance by advisers, attorneys, accountants, agents or brokers, or otherwise discouraged attendance by these professionals by charging them a costly attendance fee (as much as $1,000).

The ads and mailers often implied urgency, and that time was of the essence. They said things like: "Act Now!" "If you are over 60, you cannot afford to miss this seminar" "Seating is Limited!" "Reservations Required" "This is a time-sensitive offer!" "There is a financial storm brewing" "This is a *Must* Attend!" or "Startling presentation reveals costly mistakes that can ruin your finances."

Some ads and mailers used tactics to scare seniors into thinking that they might not be using the right investment professional, or to question their current investments. For example, they say, "If you're retired, YOU'RE A TARGET and you cannot afford to miss this workshop!" "How to Protect your Nest Egg from The Retirement *Vultures*," "Will you cause your family to split up and argue at your passing when your will or trust is read? Would you like to know how to prevent the possible breakup of your family?" and "Seniors, did you know that costly mistakes can tarnish your golden years?" These statements appear to be designed to scare vulnerable senior investors, and may help to open the door for seminar sponsors to sell unsuitable investments.

- **Seminars are designed to sell.**

While many sales seminars were advertised as "educational," "workshops," "educational dining seminar" and "nothing will be sold at this workshop," and many advertisements did not mention any investment products, all of the seminars were intended to result in product sales. They were intended ultimately to result in the attendees' opening new accounts with the sponsoring firm, and the sale of securities and other financial products. To the extent that participants may attend the seminar in order to obtain educational insights and information, they should be aware that the primary goal of the sponsors of the "free lunch" seminars is to obtain new customers and sell financial products.

Typically at a seminar, the seniors arrive at the restaurant or hotel and are shown to a private room, and to a seat. At the outset, they are usually given a questionnaire or contact card to fill out with their name, address, telephone number, and interests in particular investments or financial goals and are asked to return the card to the host. A slide show or power point presentation usually follows as drinks are served. Examiners found that the most commonly discussed products at the sales seminars were variable annuities, equity indexed annuities, real estate investment trusts, mutual funds, private placements and reverse mortgages. The food is usually not served until after the presentation is complete and the host has collected the contact information from the attendees. To ensure the attendees stay until the presentation is over, the door prizes are given last. The financial adviser speaking at the seminar also evaluates individual attendees' level of interest in opening an account and/or purchasing products.[9]

Following the seminar, seminar attendees can expect to receive additional solicitations from the firm to purchase investment products. Attendees are generally contacted by the financial adviser by telephone at least one or more times, using the contact information that the attendee provided at the seminar, and are solicited to schedule a further meeting with the financial professional and/or to open an account and purchase securities or other products. Typically, the attendee will also be added to the firm's mailing list of potential customers, and will receive additional sales materials in the mail following the sales seminar.

- **Some firms had particular compliance and supervisory controls that appeared to be effective. And, at a small number of firms (5 examinations, or 4% of the firms examined), regulators found no problems or deficiencies.**

Some examinations found that firms had specific compliance and supervisory practices that appeared to be effective in ensuring compliance with the securities laws and rules. These practices were in writing and were implemented. Particularly effective practices were those that facilitated a supervisor's advance review of the materials to be used in connection with sales seminars.

For example, one broker-dealer required its employees to forward all materials to its home office for a supervisory and compliance review prior to using them at sales seminars. Another broker-dealer utilized checklists to aid supervisors with the approval process for seminars and seminar materials. Another firm used what it called "mystery shoppers" (who were current firm employees) to attend seminars randomly to identify potential disclosure and compliance weaknesses and report back to their supervisor. These, and additional examples of effective compliance and supervisory practices found during examinations can be found in Appendix B to this report.

---

[9] At one firm, registered representatives kept a record of those who attended the seminars that included a notation of the attendees who made appointments to meet with the registered representatives after the seminar to discuss opening an account. The record also referred to those attendees who did not schedule a follow-up appointment and apparently only attended the seminar for the free lunch as "clowns."

- **Half of the examinations found that firms used advertising and sales materials that may have been misleading or exaggerated or included apparently unwarranted claims.**

The most common deficiency involved the use of potentially misleading advertising and sales literature in connection with the sales seminars. Examiners found deficiencies in 63 of the 110 examinations conducted (or 57% of the examinations conducted). Most frequently, these potentially misleading statements appeared in mailers and advertisements for the sales seminars, and involved statements about the safety, liquidity or anticipated returns of products. Additionally, some sales materials made comparisons between dissimilar investments or services, included representations about the expertise or credentials of the registered representative that appeared to be misleading or confusing, or involved testimonials that appeared to be misleading, or provided inaccurate or confusing information about the sponsoring firm.[10] Examples are described below.

⇒ *Claims about Safety, Liquidity or Returns*

Some seminar sponsors used what appeared to be misleading or exaggerated promises to lure attendees to sales seminars. For example, one advertisement for a sales seminar, called the "Senior Citizen's Retirement & Asset Protection Educational Seminar," stated, "Learn how you can earn 2-3 times more interest than what banks currently offer...*While keeping your money liquid!*" The following additional examples were found in various advertisements:

> "If you are between the ages of 65-85 join me for the most fascinating hour of your LIFE and I will show you how to immediately earn as much as $100,000, $200,000 or $300,000 . . . or more with the stroke of a pen," and "How to **guarantee** your IRA will <u>never</u> run out, regardless of market fluctuations."

> "Learn how to pass all of your assets on to your heirs while making sure the IRS gets only what you want them to have."

> "Immediately add $100,000 to your net worth"

> "You'll learn how to generate returns starting at 40% while your capital is held in an FDIC insured account."

> "How to receive a 13.3% return"

---

[10] Specifically, in 41 of the 110 examinations (or 37%), firms may have made false, misleading, exaggerated or unwarranted statements or claims; and in 29 examinations (or 26%), the firm did not appear to provide a sound basis for evaluating the statements that were made. In addition, two firms appear to have made exaggerated or unwarranted claims, opinions, or forecasts related to the performance of securities, and an additional seven made comparisons in their advertisements and/or sales literature between investments or services, but did not disclose material differences between the investments or services.

"How $100K can pay 1 Million Dollars to Your Heirs"

"Get double digit growth potential with no risk of loss and no fees"

"Your deposit plus all gains are insured 100% without limit."

Advertisements like these seemed designed to attract attention by using exaggerated and potentially misleading claims. Examiners noted that seminar sponsors may be competing with each other for attendees, particularly in local areas with large populations of retirees, and may use hyperbolic and exaggerated ads in order to "stand out" from other seminar sponsors.

⇒ *Use of Testimonials*

Examiners found that some firms used testimonials from satisfied customers as part of their sales materials and presentations at sales seminars. Examiners observed that firms sometimes used testimonials by seniors who attested to the quality of service or the investments offered by the firm in their marketing efforts to other seniors as prospective customers.

As described above in this report, to protect investors from being misled by testimonials, broker-dealers must prominently disclose that the testimonial may not be representative of the experience of other customers, the testimonial may not be indicative of future performance or success, and if more than a nominal sum is paid, broker-dealers must disclose that it is a paid testimonial (under NASD Conduct Rule 2210(d)(2)(A) and NYSE Rule 472(i)(7)). Investment advisers registered with the SEC may not use testimonials at all (under Rule 206(4)-1 under the Advisers Act).

Examinations found that some firms did not fully comply with these requirements. For example, one broker-dealer firm employed an older gentleman on a part-time basis to help with public relations. He also held accounts with the firm. His job was to attend seminars, state that he was a current customer of the firm, and stand up and give unsolicited testimonials as to the quality of the firm and its investment management. He did not disclose that he was paid to provide the testimonial, that his experience may not be representative of other customers' experience, and is not indicative of future performance or success (as required under SRO rules).

The same firm invited its current customers to its sales seminars -- to receive a free meal -- and to provide impromptu testimonials to other attendees, *e.g.*: "I am happy with the account and the returns" and "It feels like being part of a family." These testimonials did not include disclosures that these customers' experience may not be representative of other customers' experience, and is not indicative of future performance or success (as required under SRO rules).

Other testimonials identified in the examinations included:

"The [broker-dealer] puts client's best interest first."

"You can trust [the broker-dealer]."

"[I] like the approach to asset allocation which leads to broad diversification."

⇒ *Representations about the Expertise of the Financial Adviser*

Often, the advertising for sales seminars has a personal appeal and focuses on the individual person who is presenting the seminar. The advertisements frequently include a photograph of the seminar host and a description of that individual's background as an expert in providing financial advice, as well as highlighting his/her involvement in the local community. While examiners did not investigate the accuracy of all of the representations made about the background or expertise of the persons presenting the seminars, we found a few indications that information provided about the experience or the expertise of the presenter could be confusing or misleading to an attendee.

For example, two individuals distributed sales literature during a seminar that included a "team profile" of themselves as hosts of the seminar. The profile stated that one of the representatives used technical knowledge to develop an advanced mutual fund selection system combining various services and numerous data bases. Examination staff discovered that an off-the-shelf software program was used to identify potential mutual fund investments.

In other cases, individuals presenting seminars called themselves a "*Certified Senior Advisor,*" or "*Elder Care Asset Protection Specialist*" or "*Chartered Retirement Planning Counselor*" -- terms that suggest that the financial professional has some type of special credential or certification from a regulatory authority, when in fact there is no regulatory qualification or registration that recognizes such special expertise.[11] The use of these titles may be confusing or misleading to the public.

---

[11] Regulators have warned that seniors may be confused by designations that imply some expertise in providing services to seniors. NASAA's Investor Alert is available at http://www.nasaa.org/NASAA_Newsroom/Current_NASAA_Headlines/4028.cfm. The SEC has provided information on professional designations, available at http://www.sec.gov/investor/pubs/senior-profdes.htm. Additionally, FINRA provides a list of professional designations and describes them for informational purposes only – without recommending or endorsing any designation. This information is available at http://apps.finra.org/DataDirectory/1/prodesignations.aspx.

- **Individuals attending the sales seminars may not understand that the seminar is sponsored by an undisclosed company with a financial interest in product sales.**

As described above, the mailers and advertisements for the sales seminars often focused on the individual person who conducted the seminar, and often included the name, photograph and background information of the individual registered representative or investment adviser that is scheduled to speak at the seminar. Members of the public who attended the seminars or considered attending were not always provided with the name of the firm that was sponsoring the seminar, and may not be aware that product sponsors (e.g., mutual fund companies and insurance companies) provide funding for these seminars.

Examiners found that advertising and sales material provided to prospective attendees at the seminars did not always disclose the name of the broker-dealer or the investment adviser firm that was sponsoring the seminar. In fact, in 12 of the 110 examinations (or 11% of the examinations conducted), firms used sales literature that provided the name of the individual who presented the seminar, but not the name of the firm where the individual worked.[12] In 7 of these instances, the registered representatives used alternative names to do business and used these names in their advertising or sales literature, but did not also reflect the name of the broker-dealer firm that they worked for and that was offering the products or services. Providing the name of the firm would allow a prospective attendee to better research the sponsoring firm in deciding whether to attend a sales seminar.

In addition, seminar attendees and those who considered attending likely did not know that some seminars were paid for (in part or in whole) by product sponsors. This information is not required to be disclosed in advertisements or mailers for sales seminars. Mutual fund firms and insurance companies often reimburse broker-dealers or investment advisers for expenses when they hold sales seminars to solicit investors to purchase the mutual funds or insurance products. In these examinations, examiners found that mutual funds, insurance companies and limited partnership sponsors frequently reimbursed broker-dealers or investment advisers for the costs of putting on the sales seminars (*e.g.,* rental of space, the food and beverages provided, publications, advertising expenses and other free items provided to attendees). Attendees likely did not know that the sponsors of the products discussed at the seminar had paid for the costs of the seminar. In these situations, seminar attendees may not have known that the financial adviser speaking at the seminar was not unbiased in making product recommendations.

---

[12] Broker-dealers are required to reflect the name of the firm offering products and services in any advertisements or sales literature offering products or services. The name of the member must be prominently disclosed, and may also include a fictional name by which the member is commonly recognized or which is required by any state or jurisdiction (under NASD Conduct Rule 2210(d)(2)(c)(i) and (iii)).

While seminar attendees and those considering whether to attend likely were not aware that the seminar may have been paid for by a product sponsor, if a person attending a seminar purchases a security, they are required to receive relevant disclosure. Broker-dealers and investment advisers are required to disclose certain basic terms of the transaction to the customer or client, such as any payments they receive from third parties.[13] Most frequently, these disclosures are contained in the prospectus for the mutual fund or other product, or in the investment adviser's brochure (or in its Form ADV).[14]

Examinations found that, when customers purchased a security as a result of a seminar, firms provided disclosure that they received compensation from a product sponsor in the prospectus, in a statement of additional information, or in a separate disclosure form. However, in 8 examinations, the disclosure that firms provided in the prospectus stated that the firm *"may"* receive compensation from product sponsors based on assets under management, when, in fact the firm had actually received and was receiving such payments and reimbursements for seminar costs.

For example, examinations found that two broker-dealers had agreements with insurance companies under which the insurance companies paid the broker-dealers to sell their products (often called "revenue-sharing agreements"). With respect to one of these broker-dealers, most of its overall yearly sales were of the variable annuity products of a small number of insurance companies. It maintained compensation agreements with those insurance companies based on the sales that it made, and its customers' variable annuity assets that were held in their accounts with the broker-dealer for a certain length of time. The firm disclosed to investors that it "may" receive additional payments based on assets under management; however, it actually received over $1 million a year from these insurance companies, a significant amount of money for the firm based on its size.

Examinations also identified an instance of double-billing -- a registered representative obtained reimbursement for the same sales seminar expenses from multiple mutual funds. The registered representative had submitted the same restaurant bill to multiple mutual fund companies and received full payment from each of them.

---

[13] Broker-dealers must disclose the source and amount of any remuneration received or to be received from third parties in connection with a transaction under Rule 10b-10 under the Exchange Act. Advisers must make similar disclosures, generally under Section 206 of the Advisers Act, and in Form ADV Part II.

[14] "[I]n the case of offerings registered under the Securities Act of 1933, the final prospectus delivered to the customer should generally set forth the information required by the proviso with respect to source and amount of remuneration. . . . In such situations the information specified in the proviso need not be separately set forth in the confirmation." Exchange Act Release No. 13508 (May 5, 1977) at n. 41.

- **Many broker-dealer firms did not submit sales materials to NASD for review as required.**

As described earlier in this report, to help ensure that communications by broker-dealers to the public are fair, balanced and not misleading, broker-dealers must provide certain sales material to NASD's Department of Advertising Regulation for review (now, this function is performed by FINRA's Department of Advertising Regulation). Advertisements and sales literature concerning mutual funds and variable annuities must be submitted for review within 10 business days of first use or publication (NASD Rule 2210(c)(2)(A)).

These examinations found that many firms did not submit materials to NASD as required. Specifically, NASD's Advertising Regulation Department reviewed all the advertisements and sales literature collected in these examinations that were used by NASD member firms or their associated persons. This review found that 31 broker-dealer firms had failed to submit their advertising and sales literature to NASD as required. If these materials had been submitted for review, it is likely that the firms would have been advised of potentially misleading or exaggerated statements or other concerns.

- **Many examinations found indications that firms had poorly supervised these sales seminars.**

One of the most frequent deficiencies cited during the examinations was inadequate supervision of employees who held sales seminars. Examiners found weak supervision during 65 of the 110 (or 59%) examinations conducted. In the other 45 examinations, firms appeared to have implemented adequate supervisory controls over sales seminars.

During the 65 examinations in which deficiencies were found, examiners identified 102 instances in which firms did not appear to have supervised their employees in a manner that was consistent with supervisory requirements under the securities laws and SRO rules. A frequently found problem was that firms had either not established supervisory procedures, or had established procedures but did not put systems in place to properly supervise their employees who held sales seminars consistent with those procedures (in 44 of the 110 examinations, or 40%).

Examinations found deficiencies in several areas. These included: (1) a lack of written policies and procedures to address compensation received by the firm or its employees from issuers for selling the issuers' products; (2) a lack of written policies and procedures relating to the sales literature used at sales seminars; (3) not reviewing or approving materials provided to potential investors at sales seminars; (4) not reviewing incoming and outgoing correspondence; and (5) not adequately supervising branch managers who themselves sold securities to customers, and held sales seminars. Some examples follow.

⇒ *Lack of Policies and Procedures with Respect to Sales Seminars*

Examinations revealed many instances in which firms did not have specific policies and procedures with respect to sales seminars and/or communications with the public. Some firms did not require that all materials used to advertise the sales seminars, or used at the sales seminars be reviewed and approved by a supervisor prior to use. While it is impossible to determine what the outcome would have been had these firms had supervisory procedures in place, because these firms lacked supervisory procedures, it appears they did not provide adequate supervision over sales seminars. This lack of supervision may have allowed potentially exaggerated claims and misrepresentations to be made (which are described elsewhere in this report), and to go undetected by the firm's supervisors.

For example, a firm did not have procedures to monitor effectively the activities of employees in its branch offices concerning their communications with the public. Although the firm's managers knew that employees were conducting seminars, the firm did not have procedures that required that supervisors receive and approve in advance all of the sales literature that its employees distributed to the public. Other examples follow:

- A branch office did not maintain documentation evidencing approval for its registered representatives to hold sales seminars, or approval of the materials used. Dozens of sales seminars were held.

- A branch manager who maintained his own customer accounts (*aka*, a "producing" branch manager) conducted and approved his own seminars, and did not obtain review or approval by his supervisor.

- A firm's advertisement touted a 38% rate of return without any risk. When examiners requested a copy of the firm's approval of the advertisement, it could not be provided, suggesting a lack of supervision.

In a number of instances, examiners found deficiencies relating to the supervisory review of correspondence.[15] For example, at one broker-dealer firm, examiners found that 2 letters from customers authorizing the transfer of securities and funds had been altered. Specifically, the account numbers had been changed without evidence of customer approval. This could have been indicative of a possible attempt at theft. A registered principal had reviewed the correspondence, but failed to do anything about the alteration or even request an explanation as to why it was altered.

---

[15] In addition to the general requirement to establish, maintain, and enforce written supervisory procedures, broker-dealers must also establish procedures for the review and endorsement by a registered principal, of incoming and outgoing written and electronic correspondence of its registered representatives with the public (NASD Rule 3010(d)(1)). These procedures must be in writing and be designed to reasonably supervise each registered representative. Firms' processes must include methods of control over receipt and delivery of hard copy correspondence, communications received through facsimile transmissions and email (NYSE Rule 342.16 and 342.17 also address the review and approval of communications with the public).

At the outset of these examinations, regulators were concerned about the possibility that registered representatives or investment advisers may be holding sales seminars and selling products outside of their firms' supervisory controls. Thus, examiners paid particular attention to this issue.

To help ensure that broker-dealer firms can provide adequate supervision for the protection of investors, SRO rules address the business activities that can be performed by firm employees "outside" of their employment with a broker-dealer. These rules require that the employee provide notice to the firm, and the firm may also require approval of the employees' outside business activities (NASD Rule 3030 and NYSE Rule 346(b)).

Investment advisers registered with the SEC must implement policies and procedures reasonably designed to prevent violations of the Advisers Act by any of the adviser's supervised persons, including partners, officers, directors or employees of the investment adviser, or other person who provides investment advice on behalf of the investment adviser and is subject to the supervision and control of the investment adviser (under Rules 206(4)-7 and 202(a)(25) of the Advisers Act).

Most of the broker-dealer firms examined had procedures in place that addressed the outside business activities of employees. However, some firms had not actually implemented their own policies and procedures. For example, one firm required all of its registered representatives to complete a questionnaire on an annual basis disclosing their outside business activities. Its policies then required supervisory follow-up on certain outside business activities. In practice, however, the firm did not conduct any follow-up after its employees provided information about their outside activities.

Examinations also found a number of instances in which registered representatives and investment advisers hosted sales seminars and were ultimately selling investment products to the attendees of the seminars without their firms' knowledge of the seminars themselves. The registered representatives and investment advisers incorrectly considered these seminars to be "outside business activities," and thus outside the supervision and compliance controls of the firms. At one firm, for example, a registered representative, who was also a mortgage broker, hosted seminars on the subject of mortgages and then also sold securities products to the seminar attendees. These seminars were not supervised by his firm.

- **Some examinations found indications that registered representatives or investment advisers holding the sales seminars had recommended investments that did not appear to be suitable for the individual customers/clients.**

As described in this report, sales seminars are often used to attract new customers and clients. When opening a new account, customers complete a new account form with a broker-dealer, or sign an investment advisory contract with an investment adviser. As part of this process, a broker-dealer or investment advisory firm will obtain information about the customer/client and his/her investment objectives, risk tolerance, time horizon for investments, and overall investment needs. This information assists the firm in ensuring that the recommendations made are suitable for the particular customer or client in light of their age, income, net worth, investment experience and risk tolerance. The determination about whether a particular investment product is suitable is based on the particular investor and his or her individual investment objectives.

During each examination, examiners reviewed account documents and other information maintained by the firm about a sample of customers to evaluate whether the investments that were recommended to customers appeared to be suitable. Examiners' primary focus was on accounts that were opened by attendees at the seminars, though examiners also reviewed other accounts when appropriate.

In some examinations, examiners found indications that apparently unsuitable recommendations to purchase investments were made at the sales seminars, or following the seminars, when an attendee opened an account. Examiners had concerns about the suitability of products recommended in 25 of the 110 exams conducted, or in 23% of the examinations conducted.

Examiners noted concern that some firms may not be adequately considering the individual needs and circumstances of each customer when determining whether a product was suitable for that customer. For example, at one broker-dealer, examiners noted that the same investment objective was identified on almost every new account form in one branch. Despite differences in the customers' ages, net worth, income levels and investment experience, almost every new account form indicated that the customers had "growth" and "growth with income" as their investment objectives. Almost every customer was invested in the same annuity product, and in the same three sub-accounts. These investments suggest that all customers were treated the same way when the firm was recommending investments, instead of in accordance with their unique needs in light of the variances in their ages, net worth, incomes, and investment experiences. At another broker-dealer, examiners noted four senior investors whose stated incomes and net worth did not meet the requirements of the products they were sold.

Examiners also found situations in which specific products and types of accounts were recommended to individual seniors, which may have been unsuitable or inappropriate for these particular customers. We note that these products and accounts are suitable and appropriate for some investors, but are not suitable and appropriate for others in light of their investment objectives, the time horizon for investment, or the risk involved. Examples follow.

⇒ *Variable Annuities*

Variable annuities are generally considered long-term investment vehicles, and therefore, the investor's time horizon for holding the investment and the investor's liquidity needs are particularly relevant in determining whether it is a suitable investment. Also relevant is whether the investor already holds a variable annuity investment, and whether the various features and costs make the product suitable in light of the investors' existing holdings. In particular, firms are required to ensure that a new variable annuity is suitable when recommending that an existing variable product be "exchanged" for a new one. A replacement that doesn't improve the customer's existing position, and that is designed merely to generate new sales commissions, would be prohibited by NASD rules (Rule IM-2310.2).[16]

At one firm, a review of account records for a sample of customers who had purchased a variable annuity based on the firm's recommendations indicated that 66% of the customers had sold a variable annuity in order to purchase a new one, and that most of the customers had investment time horizons of 3-5 years or less (including some with horizons of 1-3 years). Because of the significant surrender fees that are charged to customers who sell their variable annuities within a certain time-frame (usually within seven years of purchase), these products did not appear to be suitable for these customers.

At another firm, a registered representative recommended that a customer invest approximately 80% of his stated net worth in variable annuities. To finance the purchase of these variable annuities, the registered representative recommended that the customer sell his existing investments that were providing greater diversification, liquidity and annual income to his portfolio. The customer's previous portfolio holdings also included a variable annuity with a death benefit valued at over $30,000, income-producing investments such as investment grade corporate bonds, preferred stock, and money market funds. Based on the customer's other diversified portfolio holdings, and the customer's investment objectives of growth and income, the recommendation to sell virtually all of the customer's assets and purchase a variable annuity appeared to be unsuitable.

⇒ *Real Estate Investment Trusts*

At one firm, examiners found that registered representatives recommended that customers with a conservative investment objective and risk tolerance invest in a real estate investment trust, which was an illiquid and speculative investment. The prospectus for the investment stated that "these investments entail a high degree of risk, are long term investments and are suitable if investors have no immediate need for liquidity or can bear the complete loss of the investment." Because of the lack of liquidity, high degree of risk and long term nature of the investment, these investments appeared to be unsuitable for customers with conservative investment objectives.

---

[16]   *"NASD Regulation Reminds Members And Associated Persons That Sales of Variable Contracts Are Subject to NASD Suitability Requirements"* (Oct. 1989) NASD Notice to Members 96-86, available at:
http://www.finra.org/web/groups/rules_regs/documents/notice_to_members/p004697.pdf
FINRA has proposed a new rule that would create requirements for recommendations, review by a principal, and supervisory and training requirements tailored specifically to transactions in deferred variable annuities (proposed Rule 2821).

⇒ *Low-rated Municipal Bonds*

At one firm, a registered representative recommended that two senior investors with conservative investment objectives purchase non-rated and low-rated municipal bonds. One investor purchased multiple issues that subsequently went into default or that failed to pay interest. The non-rated municipal bonds represented approximately 80% of her stated liquid net worth. In another instance, a retired over 70 year old investor with a primary objective of income and a liquid net worth of between $25,000 and $49,999 had the majority of his liquid net worth invested in non-investment grade speculative bonds. These investments may not have been suitable for these customers.

⇒ *Collateralized Mortgage Obligations*

At one firm, several registered representatives had recommended that customers with conservative investment objectives purchase certain collateralized mortgage obligations (CMOs) with high degrees of risk (based on the particular tranches being sold). In some cases, the customer accounts used high percentages of margin to purchase the securities. In addition, these CMO positions were being actively traded in the customer accounts, generating significant commissions for the registered representatives involved. These transactions appeared to be unsuitable for the particular customers involved.

⇒ *Fee-Based Accounts*

Financial services firms offer different types of accounts to customers. In particular, in recent years, fee-based accounts have become a popular account choice, and have been offered by broker-dealers and investment advisers. In a fee-based account, a customer pays a fee based on the amount of assets in the account. In a commission-based account, a customer pays a commission charge on each transaction.[17]

Prior to opening a fee-based account for a customer, a broker-dealer must have reasonable grounds to believe that such an account is appropriate for that particular customer (under NASD NTM 03-68 and NYSE Rule 405A). In addition, broker-dealers must disclose all material components of the fee-based program to the customer, including the fee schedule, the services provided and the fact that the program may cost more than paying for the services separately (under NASD NTM 03-68). It may be inappropriate to place a customer in an account with a fee structure that reasonably can be expected to result in a greater cost than an alternative account offered by the firm (under NASD NTM 03-68, NYSE Rule 405A).

---

[17]   In a recent decision, the Court of Appeals for the District of Columbia Circuit vacated Rule 202(a)(11)-1 under the Advisers Act, which provided, among other things, that fee-based brokerage accounts were not advisory accounts and were thus not subject to the Advisers Act. Financial Planning Ass'n v. SEC, 2007 U.S. App. LEXIS 7356, 482 F.3d 481 (D.C. Cir. 2007).

Examiners found indications that fee-based accounts may have been recommended to customers for whom they may not have been appropriate. At one firm, a registered representative recommended a fee-based account to a senior investor. The account charged a fee of 1.838% of assets under management. This customer's account had no transactions, and held three variable annuities, which had separate, total internal management costs of approximately 3% of the assets. The customer was being charged two levels of fees on the same assets, once by the insurance company for management fees and again by the broker-dealer for the account fee. This type of account may not have been appropriate for this particular customer, in light of her investment objectives and the portfolio holdings.

⇒ *Recommendations that Customers Use Equity from their Homes*

Regulators have urged caution about recommendations that investors, especially senior investors, obtain loans on their homes in order to finance the purchase of securities. By doing so, customers may suffer investment losses that could result in their inability to pay off the loans on their homes, and ultimately, risk the loss of their homes altogether.[18]

In one examination, an investment adviser had recommended that senior investors obtain mortgages or refinance their homes and liquidate their existing retirement accounts, in order to purchase equity-indexed universal life insurance (EIUL) policies. This investment strategy speculated that the rate of return earned on the EIUL policy would exceed the cost of the new mortgage on the client's home. Dozens of senior investors followed this advice and effectively mortgaged 100% of the value of their homes. This type of investment strategy may not have been suitable for individuals on a fixed income because if the market index failed to perform, the policy provided a low return, and the client remained responsible for the annual mortgage cost and insurance premiums associated with the EIUL policy. In addition, the adviser's seminar materials only provided a positive analysis of potential returns that could be earned by clients and did not appear to offer discussion of any risk factors in using this investment strategy. This may have been an unsuitable high-risk investment strategy for these clients.

- **In some instances, the sales seminars may have involved fraud.**

Examiners found indications of possible fraudulent practices in 14 examinations (or 13% of the examinations conducted). These involved potentially egregious misrepresentations of risk and return, liquidation of accounts without the customer's knowledge or consent, and sales of fictitious investment notes. Some instances of apparent fraud are described below. In total, 25 of the 110 examinations (or 23%) are under review for possible further investigation or action by a state, FINRA or SEC.[19]

---

[18] *See* NASD Investor Alert, *Betting the Ranch: Risking Your Home to Buy Securities* (March 15, 2004), available at http://www.finra.org/InvestorInformation/InvestorAlerts/MarginandBorrowing/BettingtheRanchRiskingYourHometoBuySecurities/P005961; NASD Notice to Members 04-89, *available at* http://www.finra.org/RulesRegulation/NoticestoMembers/2004NoticestoMembers/P012715.

[19] Many examinations had multiple dispositions. For example, a deficiency letter may have been

It is important to note that the types of potentially fraudulent conduct identified in these examinations are not limited to sales seminars; rather, the types of potential frauds described below are similar to the types of fraud perpetuated against seniors and other types of investors through means other than sales seminars. Indeed, securities regulators have brought numerous enforcement actions involving these types of frauds.[20]

⇒ *Possible Misrepresentations about Risk and Expected Returns*

Several examinations uncovered instances where registered representatives or investment advisers may have overstated the potential benefits of a product or failed to disclose important risks for investors. In one instance, for example, the firm's seminar advertisement indicated that customers could earn up to a 38% rate of return without any risk, and incorrectly implied that fixed annuities were guaranteed by the government.

⇒ *Liquidating Accounts Without Investor Knowledge or Consent*

In another examination, examiners found that an investment adviser had liquidated clients' investments and used the proceeds to purchase potentially unsuitable investments apparently without the client's knowledge or consent. The investment adviser conducted seniors-only seminars at hotels, offering retirees free breakfast and financial advice. He used marketing materials that claimed to teach seniors how to eliminate taxes on IRA accounts, reduce or eliminate taxes on social security income, and increase yields on investments from 20% to 300%. After the seminars, the investment adviser scheduled one-on-one meetings with interested individuals on the pretext of preparing a financial plan for them. During these meetings, the investment adviser may have misled seniors into signing several blank authorization forms, claiming that he needed the forms to obtain additional financial information. Instead, the financial plans appear not to have

---

provided to the firm requesting corrective action, and findings from that exam may also have been referred for possible disciplinary or enforcement action.

[20] *See, e.g.,* SEC v. C. Wesley Rhodes, Jr., et al., SEC Lit. Rel. No. 20144 (June 5, 2007) (defendants allegedly defrauded seniors of $38 million by misrepresenting stock and bond purchases); SEC v. One Wall Street, Inc, et al, SEC Lit. Rel. No. 20123 (May 22, 2007) (defendants allegedly defrauded seniors of at least $1.6 million through false and misleading statements regarding investment risks); SEC v. Empire Development Group, et al., SEC Lit. Rel. No. 20122 (May 18, 2007) (defendants allegedly defrauded unsuspecting senior investors with limited means of nearly $2 million through the sale of unregistered securities in bogus real estate development companies); *Citigroup Global Markets to Pay Over $15 Million to Settle Charges Relating to Misleading Documents and Inadequate Disclosure in Retirement Seminars, Meetings for BellSouth Employees*, FINRA News Release (June 6, 2007), *available at* http://www.finra.org/PressRoom/NewsReleases/2007NewsReleases/P019240; *NASD Investor Alert Warns Workers About Early Retirement Investment Pitches*, FINRA News Release (Sept. 14, 2006), *available at* http://www.finra.org/PressRoom/NewsReleases/2006NewsReleases/P017386; *Kenneth Edward Stephens*, Decision 06-216, 2006 WL 3900166 (N.Y.S.E. Hearing Board December 13, 2006) (defendant allegedly defrauded seniors of over $1.3 million through unauthorized trading); *David A. Noyes & Co., Inc.*, Decision 05-98, 2005 WL 3439785 (N.Y.S.E. Hearing Panel November 9, 2005) (defendant allegedly made unsuitable sales of variable annuities to unsuspecting seniors resulting in a loss of approximately $375,000).

been created, and it appears that the investment adviser later completed the forms in order to liquidate the clients' existing portfolios and purchase equity-indexed annuities, without the knowledge, authorization, or consent of each of the clients.

⇒ *Possible Fraud in the Sale of Oil and Gas Partnerships*

At one firm, examiners discovered that the broker-dealer was involved in an apparent scheme that targeted elderly investors by selling unsuitable, unregistered oil and gas partnerships. The partnerships were sold through sales seminars. As part of this scheme, it appears that investors' funds may have been misappropriated. It also appears that the broker-dealer may have made misrepresentations regarding the risks involved with these partnerships, stating that they were safe investments that would generate an income of 10-12%, with minimal risk. It appears that approximately $10 million was raised from dozens of elderly retired investors. This registered representative may have made material misrepresentations and omissions to investors concerning the value, nature and/or disposition of their purported investments by reflecting the market value of these partnerships as the original principal invested. The market value was not ascertainable because a ready market did not exist for such securities.

⇒ *Sales of Fictitious "Notes"*

At another firm, examiners found indications that a registered representative, who conducted business out of a retirement community, may have sold a non-existent investment to a senior investor for approximately $10,000. The investor was told that her money would be loaned to real estate developers, when the money may have been used for personal expenses of the registered representative, mostly to repay trading losses he had incurred years prior, as well as interest on those losses.

V.   CONCLUSION

The results of these examinations lead regulators to conclude that financial services firms should take steps to supervise sales seminars more closely, and specifically take steps to review and approve all advertisements and sales materials for accuracy and to ensure that they do not contain exaggerated or misleading claims. In addition, firms should redouble efforts to ensure that the investment recommendations they make to seniors are suitable in light of the particular customer's investment objectives. With the growing senior demographic, firms might consider specific training for their registered representatives and investment advisers regarding sales to senior investors.

Regulators have compiled a list of supervisory practices that have been identified during examinations and that appeared to be effective, which is included in Appendix B of this report. This information may assist firms in considering their own supervisory practices with respect to sales seminars. Regulators further urge financial services firms to take steps to assure that supervisory procedures with respect to sales seminars are being implemented effectively.

Regulators participating in these examinations will continue to focus examination, enforcement and regulatory efforts on the use of sales seminars targeted to seniors.

In addition, regulators conclude that, because seniors are targeted as attendees for sales seminars, ongoing investor education efforts for seniors should provide education with respect to "free lunch" sales seminars. Specifically, senior investors should understand that these are *sales* seminars -- that is, they are intended to result in the sales of financial products, and they may be sponsored by an undisclosed company with a financial interest in product sales. Investor education efforts should emphasize that, despite the claims of urgency that are sometimes made by sponsors of sales seminars, and in light of the possibility of misleading or exaggerated statements or claims about investment products or the expertise of the financial adviser, investors should take time to research the firm, the financial adviser as well as the product being offered before opening an account or making a purchase. Regulators make a variety of tools available to investors to assist them in understanding investment products and investigating a broker or other financial professional before investing, and many of these tools are listed in Appendix C to this report.

###

APPENDIX A

SAMPLE ADVERTISEMENTS

This appendix contains a sample of advertisements (many of which appeared in local newspapers and mass-mailed invitations) soliciting attendance at sales seminars. They are included as illustrative examples of the types of advertisements commonly used. Including them in this report does not indicate that they contain either accurate or inaccurate statements. The names of the sponsors, addresses, telephone numbers and other identifying information have been redacted.

FREE FOOD.
FREE GOLF.
FREE DRINKS.

It doesn't get any better than this!

JOIN US FOR GOLF NIGHT
TUESDAY, MARCH 14, 2006

Enjoy a beautiful sunset!

Enjoy a complimentary gourmet dinner!

Enjoy an open bar!

And...

A special presentation on advanced estate and financial strategies for wealth retirees ages 70-85. This presentation is appropriate for those with a net worth of $3 million or more. It will be held at the finest penthouse office in all of South Florida — ▬▬▬▬▬▬▬▬▬

Attendees will receive...

- Priceless information
- An incredible dining experience
- A free sleeve of Titleist, Callaway or Nike golf balls
- A chance to win a free set of Callaway golf clubs

Presentation begins at 5pm...

- Followed by gourmet dinner
- An incredible sunset
- And free golf equipment

SEATING AVAILABLE TO FIRST 40 CALLERS. PLEASE RSVP 1-888-▬▬▬▬

The Experts in Retirement Income Planning

This appendix contains a sample of advertisements (many of which appeared in local newspapers and mass-mailed invitations) soliciting attendance at sales seminars. They are included as illustrative examples of the types of advertisements commonly used. Including them in this report does not indicate that they contain either accurate or inaccurate statements. The names of the sponsors, addresses, telephone numbers and other identifying information have been redacted.

How To Avoid the Costly Mistakes That Cause Retirees to Lose Their Financial Independence

8 Strategies to Protect Your Financial Security

We are conducting an informational workshop that covers many topics related to your retirement. NO, this is not another presentation by your local brokerage firm about investing. **There will be nothing sold at this workshop.** Our speaker will inform you about recent changes in Federal and State laws and show you how to avoid the biggest financial mistakes seniors make.

I would like to personally **invite you and up to three guests** to attend this workshop designed exclusively for seniors. As usual, when the government changes laws that apply to you, they do not personally notify you. You will learn about...

- **TAXES:** Lower or eliminate taxes on Social Security, Interest Income, Capital Gains, and taxes upon death.

- **INCOME:** Learn the techniques to increase your spendable income.

- **PROBATE:** Become aware of critical facts regarding Trusts and Lawsuits.

- **TOD and POD:** Learn how these can benefit seniors.

- **S-T-R-E-T-C-H IRAs:** How to prevent your IRA from becoming an Internal Revenue Account upon death.

- **ANNUITIES:** What are the Pros and Cons?

- **LOST MONEY IN THE MARKET?** Learn what you can do about it!

- **NO LONG TERM CARE?** Learn how you can protect your assets from a nursing home situation without expensive insurance!

Due to the popularity of this workshop, available seating is limited and reservations are required. Please respond immediately to guarantee a seat.

Monday	**OR**	**Tuesday**
June 19, 2006		June 20, 2006
11:00 am & 3:00 pm		11:00 am
(meal following)		(meal following)

LOCATION

 *Cafeteria*

Seating is limited. To make your reservations, call Toll Free 1-877-████ (24 Hours)

PS: THE LAST WORKSHOP WAS FULL. IT COULD CHANGE YOUR LIFE!

(NOTE: LAWYERS, BROKERS, CPA'S OR ADVISORS MAY NOT ATTEND AS SPACE IS NEEDED FOR SENIORS.)

The presenter, speaker and sponsor of this information is a licensed, independent Insurance agent. The presenter, speaker and sponsor of this information (Invitation) as well as the information presented at the seminar is not related to, endorsed by, nor connected with and not approved by any Government Agency or organization. Although the seminar is providing information of value for consumers, the seminar is a solicitation for Insurance products such as Medicare supplements, Long Term Care Insurance, Life Insurance & Annuities. Some of the Insurance Companies that the licensed agent represents are

---

This appendix contains a sample of advertisements (many of which appeared in local newspapers and mass-mailed invitations) soliciting attendance at sales seminars. They are included as illustrative examples of the types of advertisements commonly used. Including them in this report does not indicate that they contain either accurate or inaccurate statements. The names of the sponsors, addresses, telephone numbers and other identifying information have been redacted.

This appendix contains a sample of advertisements (many of which appeared in local newspapers and mass-mailed invitations) soliciting attendance at sales seminars. They are included as illustrative examples of the types of advertisements commonly used. Including them in this report does not indicate that they contain either accurate or inaccurate statements. The names of the sponsors, addresses, telephone numbers and other identifying information have been redacted.

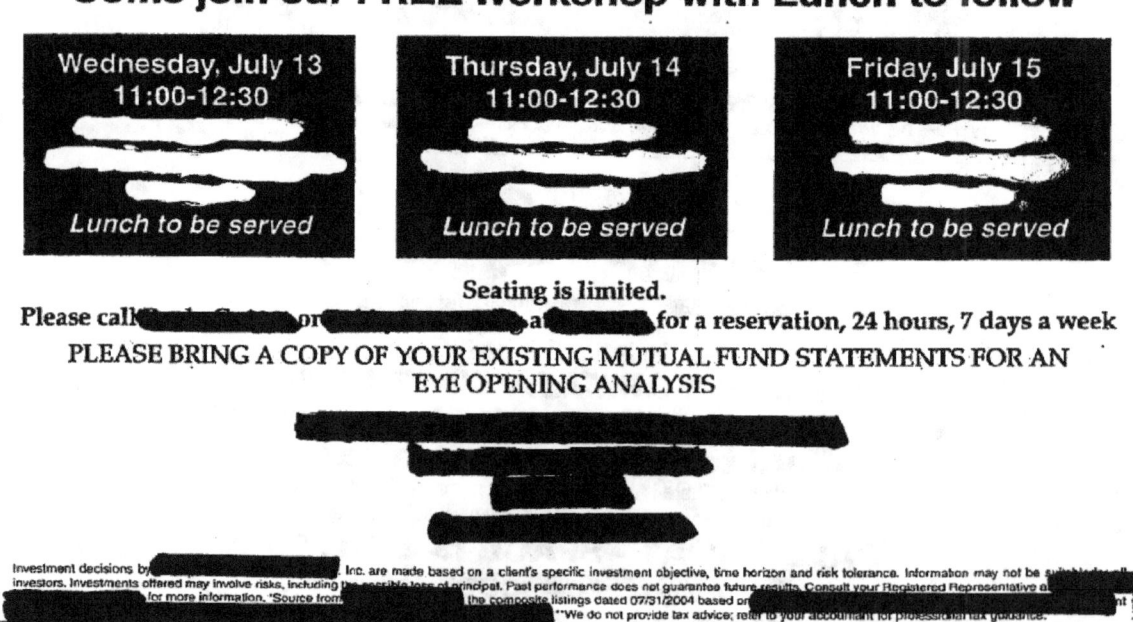

FINALLY, A DIFFERENT SEMINAR!
If you own a mutual fund you must attend!

QUESTION? Is your mutual fund really performing as well as you think?

FACT: There are Mutual Funds that have an average annual return in excess of **12%*** for the past 70 years!

Learn how we:

- Select the most consistent performers
- Explore the most cost effective means of acquiring funds
- Choose the best money managers on Wall Street
- Use methods to minimize income tax consequences**

Come join our FREE Workshop with Lunch to follow

Wednesday, July 13 11:00-12:30	Thursday, July 14 11:00-12:30	Friday, July 15 11:00-12:30
Lunch to be served	Lunch to be served	Lunch to be served

Seating is limited.

Please call ▮▮▮▮ or ▮▮▮▮ at ▮▮▮▮ for a reservation, 24 hours, 7 days a week

PLEASE BRING A COPY OF YOUR EXISTING MUTUAL FUND STATEMENTS FOR AN EYE OPENING ANALYSIS

Investment decisions by ▮▮▮▮ Inc. are made based on a client's specific investment objective, time horizon and risk tolerance. Information may not be suitable for all investors. Investments offered may involve risks, including the possible loss of principal. Past performance does not guarantee future results. Consult your Registered Representative at ▮▮▮▮ for more information. *Source from ▮▮▮▮ the composite listings dated 07/31/2004 based on ▮▮▮▮. **We do not provide tax advice; refer to your accountant for professional tax guidance.

This appendix contains a sample of advertisements (many of which appeared in local newspapers and mass-mailed invitations) soliciting attendance at sales seminars. They are included as illustrative examples of the types of advertisements commonly used. Including them in this report does not indicate that they contain either accurate or inaccurate statements. The names of the sponsors, addresses, telephone numbers and other identifying information have been redacted.

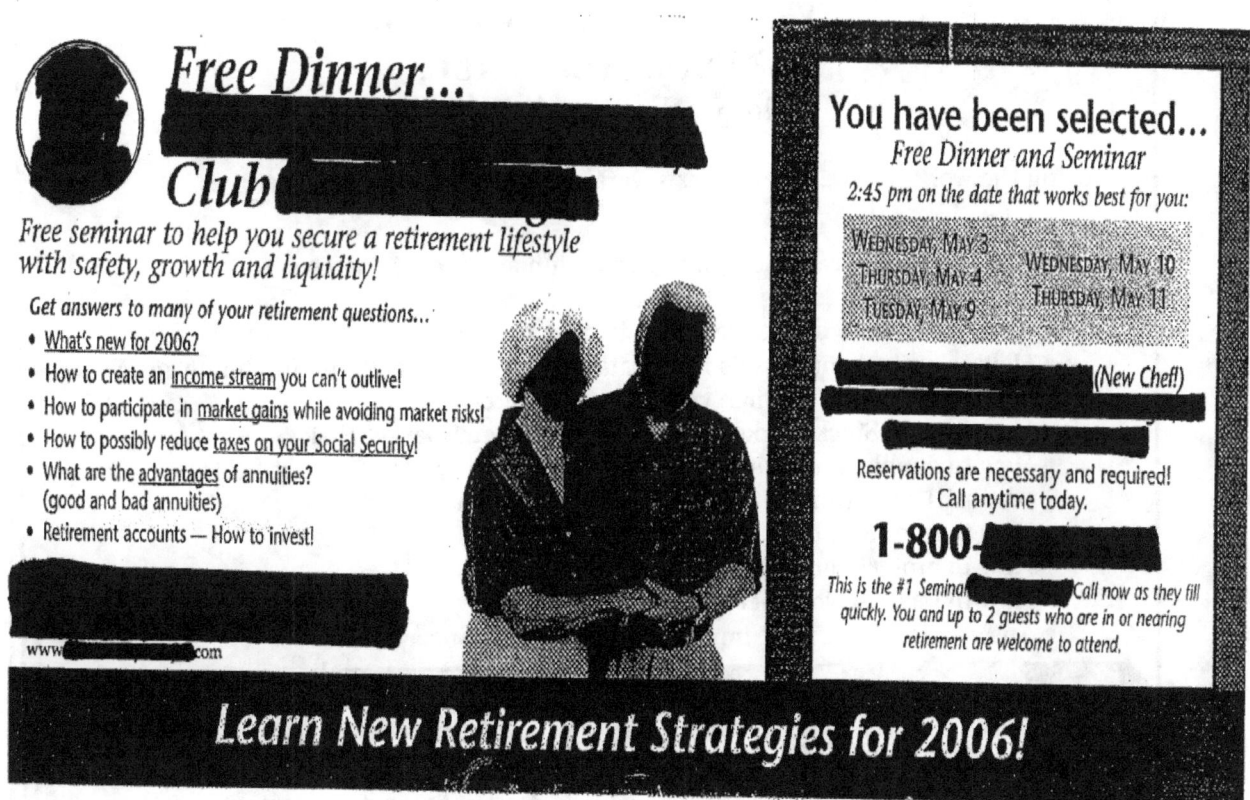

This appendix contains a sample of advertisements (many of which appeared in local newspapers and mass-mailed invitations) soliciting attendance at sales seminars. They are included as illustrative examples of the types of advertisements commonly used. Including them in this report does not indicate that they contain either accurate or inaccurate statements. The names of the sponsors, addresses, telephone numbers and other identifying information have been redacted.

Senior Financial Preservation Workshop

Are You Dissatisfied With Your Investment Performance?

If you are retired or nearing retirement, this is the one workshop you cannot afford to miss!

You and a guest are cordially invited to attend a
FREE SENIOR FINANCIAL PRESERVATION WORKSHOP.
Your lunch and program are
ABSOLUTELY FREE.
No products will be sold.

During the workshop we will discuss several areas that affect today's retirees.

Including:
- The most up to date Medicare information and recent changes
- Wills and Trusts
- Long-Term Care Insurance and is it right for you
- How to protect your assets from catastrophic illness and nursing home costs WITHOUT the high cost of long term care insurance
- How to earn Stock Market Linked Gains without Market Risk
- How to double, even triple your returns on what your CDs (certificates of deposit) are paying with no risk to your principal
- How to minimize taxes on your Social Security Income
- How to protect your assets from PROBATE
- How to increase your net worth
- Answers to YOUR most important retirement concerns

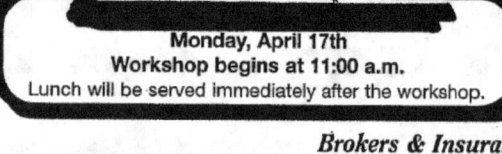

Monday, April 17th Workshop begins at 11:00 a.m. Lunch will be served immediately after the workshop.	**Monday, April 17th** Workshop begins at 2:00 p.m. Dinner will be served immediately after the workshop.

Brokers & Insurance Agents cost: $750.00

Seating is limited and reservations are required.
Call the 24-Hour seminar reservations hotline to make your reservation TODAY. Call NOW!!
TOLL FREE 1-800-███████ ext. 200

IF YOU ARE 50 OR OVER, DON'T MISS THIS FREE INFORMATION WORKSHOP!

This appendix contains a sample of advertisements (many of which appeared in local newspapers and mass-mailed invitations) soliciting attendance at sales seminars. They are included as illustrative examples of the types of advertisements commonly used. Including them in this report does not indicate that they contain either accurate or inaccurate statements. The names of the sponsors, addresses, telephone numbers and other identifying information have been redacted.

Join ▮▮▮▮▮▮▮▮▮, CFP, CLU for any of our
FREE INVESTMENT WORKSHOPS and learn how to secure
your assets and maintain your current lifestyle
throughout any economic climate.

CALL ▮▮▮-▮▮-▮▮▮ or
Toll Free at 888-▮▮▮▮▮▮
to reserve your seat today at one of these
valuable FREE LUNCHEON WORKSHOP

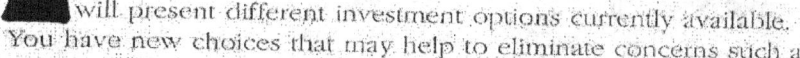

ALTERNATIVE INVESTMENT WORKSHOP
Discover the many additional investment options available to you

▮▮▮ will present different investment options currently available.
You have new choices that may help to eliminate concerns such as:
- *Losing money in the stock market*   • *Settling for low interest rates*
- *Retirement funds that may not last another 20 to 30 years*

Thursday, March 16, 10 AM to 1 PM
▮▮▮▮▮▮▮▮▮▮▮▮

Tuesday, March 21, 10 AM to 1 PM
▮▮▮▮ Steak House
▮▮▮▮▮▮▮▮

Tuesday, April 4, 10 AM to 1 PM
▮▮▮▮▮▮▮▮▮▮▮

Thursday, April 6, 10 AM to 1 PM
▮▮▮▮ Steak House
▮▮▮▮▮▮▮▮

ANNUITIES WORKSHOP
Annuities can be a valuable tool during these turbulent economic times.

During the Annuities Workshop ▮▮▮ will answer questions such as:
- *Should you invest your IRA in an annuity?*   • *Is tax deferral truly valuable?*
- *Are the guarantees offered through variable annuities valuable?*
- *Are annuities expensive?*

Thursday, March 23, 10 AM to 1 PM
▮▮▮ Resort and Club
▮▮▮▮▮▮▮

This appendix contains a sample of advertisements (many of which appeared in local newspapers and mass-mailed invitations) soliciting attendance at sales seminars. They are included as illustrative examples of the types of advertisements commonly used. Including them in this report does not indicate that they contain either accurate or inaccurate statements. The names of the sponsors, addresses, telephone numbers and other identifying information have been redacted.

_____ Cordially Invite You To Attend A Complimentary Dinner Workshop On:

FINANCIAL DEFENSE FOR SENIORS

If you're retired YOU'RE A TARGET and you cannot afford to miss this workshop!

This workshop is a broad collection of facts and circumstances intended to further educate you. Don't be fooled by workshops and seminars that focus on losing money to taxes and income increasing schemes. Often times, these seminars are geared toward funneling attendees into a single investment product that may be **very inappropriate.**

Call Today! As Seating Is Limited

TOPICS TO BE DISCUSSED:

- What the true intentions of most seminar pitches really are.
- How financial "professionals" hide fees and commissions.
- What a real vs. a phony financial designation is.
- Why 99% of local seminars are attempting to sell Equity Indexed Annuities.
- The ANNUITY BONUS SCAM!
- Why so many "Financial Planners" call themselves President, CEO and/or Vice President of whatever company they represent.
- How many seminar presenters are just insurance agents masquerading as financial planners. The average person can study for 2 weeks and become an insurance agent.
- Why a revocable trust is not a "fix all."
- Why it takes more than one person to effectively manage your finances.
- Why REAL Financial Advisors have nothing to fear and why imitators are running for cover.

The Financial Defense For Seniors Workshop is Presented by _____

_____ " Come hear facts, not smoke and mirrors - real life strategies on how to sift through the noise. This is an educational workshop with ABSOLUTELY no attempts to sell specific products. There is no cost or obligation to attend. We guarantee it will be time well spent.

Free Gourmet Meal immediately following the workshop!

DINNER	DINNER	DINNER
Tues., May 23, 2006	Wed., June 7, 2006	Wed., June 21, 2006
4:30 pm	4:30 pm	4:30 pm

Legal Counsel and Documents Prepared by.

LOCATION

_____ Art Museum

The Ethical Alternative

Spouses are urged to attend

No Brokers or Agents Admitted.

This appendix contains a sample of advertisements (many of which appeared in local newspapers and mass-mailed invitations) soliciting attendance at sales seminars. They are included as illustrative examples of the types of advertisements commonly used. Including them in this report does not indicate that they contain either accurate or inaccurate statements. The names of the sponsors, addresses, telephone numbers and other identifying information have been redacted.

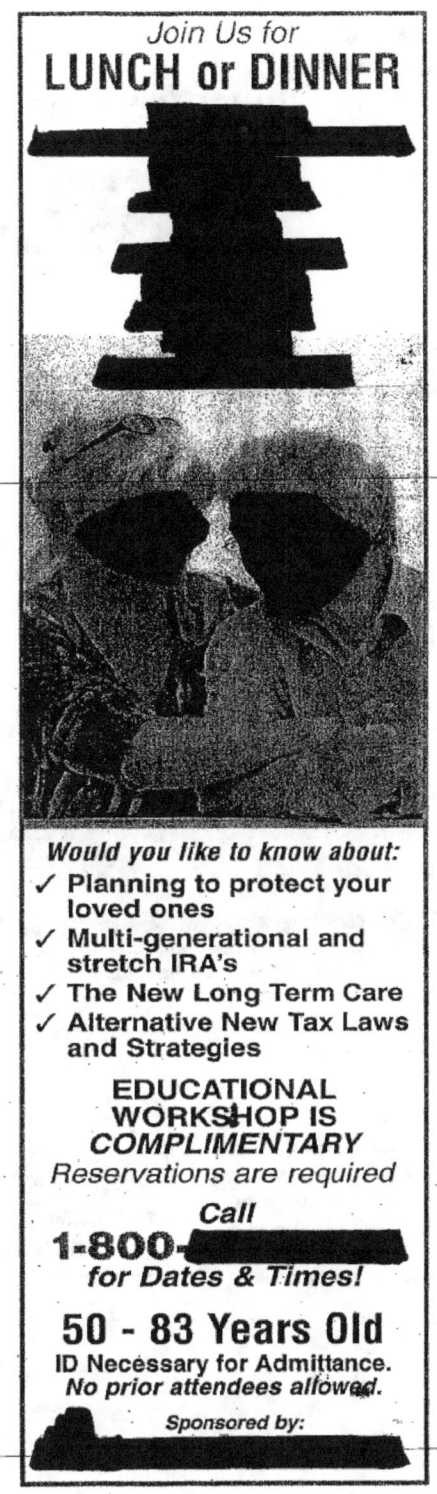

This appendix contains a sample of advertisements (many of which appeared in local newspapers and mass-mailed invitations) soliciting attendance at sales seminars. They are included as illustrative examples of the types of advertisements commonly used. Including them in this report does not indicate that they contain either accurate or inaccurate statements. The names of the sponsors, addresses, telephone numbers and other identifying information have been redacted.

Dinner Is On Us!

Senior and Veterans Dinner 2006

Dinner Is On Us!

We would like to invite you to spend <u>60 minutes</u> with The ████████ ADVISORY GROUP as our guest for dinner. This dinner is by invitation only and is intended for <u>persons age 60 and older</u> that are interested in safely investing their retirement "nest egg".

LEARN THE FOLLOWING:

* *Safety: How to avoid losses on your investments, really!*

* *Retired Veterans: You may be eligible for $1,674 per month in unknown benefits!*

* *CD Investors: How to increase your CD interest rates!*

* *Taxes: How to <u>reduce</u> taxes on your social security, bank CD interest and others!*

* *Fees: How to <u>eliminate the outrageous fees</u> on your investments!*

* *Creditors and Lawsuits: How to protect your retirement "nest egg" with one simple beneficiary form!*

* *Advanced Tax Planning: $2 Million Estates and above - eliminate capital gain taxes!*

* *Probate: How to avoid probate expenses, time delays and lawyer fees at death!*

* *IRA's and 401(k)'s: Know your options!*

Your speaker will be ████████████████████
"I enjoy helping retirees with financial decisions and protecting their retirement "nest egg". I would encourage you to attend and receive a valuable financial 2nd opinion."

As a **SPECIAL BONUS,** you will learn how you can earn a <u>guaranteed</u> 13.58% for the next 12 months.

Dinner Dates Available
Tuesday, April 18, 2006 – 3:00 p.m.
Wednesday, April 19, 2006 – 3:00 p.m.
Thursday, April 20, 2006 – 3:00 p.m.
(If married, both husband and wife should attend)
(Agents, Brokers, and Children Will Not Be Admitted)

Call
1-866-████████ (24 hrs)
Seating Is Limited And Fills Quickly

This appendix contains a sample of advertisements (many of which appeared in local newspapers and mass-mailed invitations) soliciting attendance at sales seminars. They are included as illustrative examples of the types of advertisements commonly used. Including them in this report does not indicate that they contain either accurate or inaccurate statements. The names of the sponsors, addresses, telephone numbers and other identifying information have been redacted.

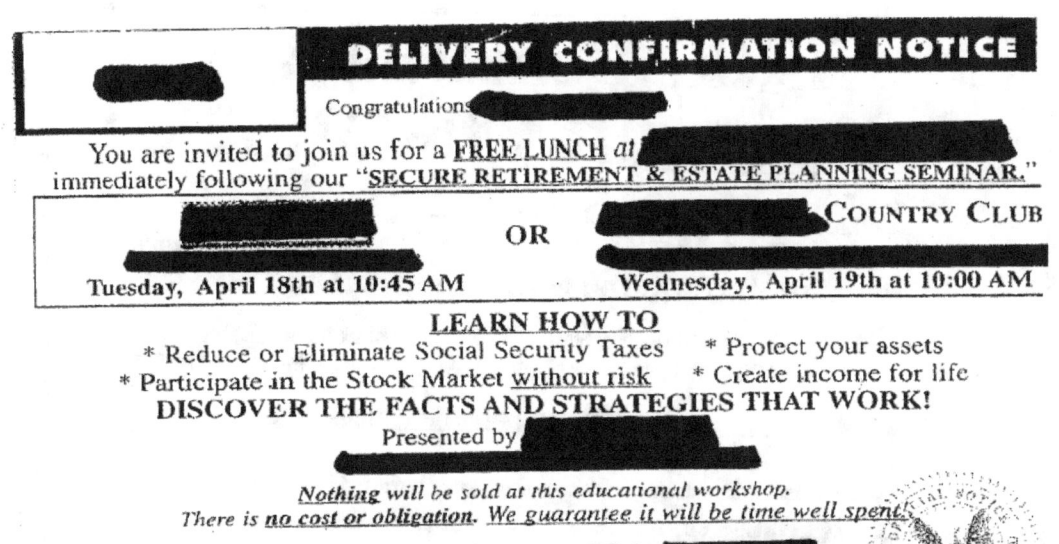

DELIVERY CONFIRMATION NOTICE

Congratulations ▓▓▓

You are invited to join us for a **FREE LUNCH** *at* ▓▓▓
immediately following our "SECURE RETIREMENT & ESTATE PLANNING SEMINAR."

▓▓▓ **OR** ▓▓▓ **COUNTRY CLUB**

▓▓▓ ▓▓▓

Tuesday, April 18th at 10:45 AM   Wednesday, April 19th at 10:00 AM

LEARN HOW TO

* Reduce or Eliminate Social Security Taxes   * Protect your assets
* Participate in the Stock Market *without risk*   * Create income for life

DISCOVER THE FACTS AND STRATEGIES THAT WORK!

Presented by ▓▓▓

*Nothing will be sold at this educational workshop.
There is no cost or obligation. We guarantee it will be time well spent.*

Please RSVP to 1-800-▓▓▓

All spouses are urged to attend. You may also invite a guest!

Call now, seating is limited!   **Free Lunch!**

PLEASE RSVP

FREE
Lunch at:

▓▓▓

Tuesday, April 18th at 10:45am

or

▓▓▓

COUNTRY CLUB
Wednesday, April 19th at 10:00am

PRESORTED
FIRST CLASS
US POSTAGE
PAID
TAMPA, FL
PERMIT #78

COMPANY

STREET ADDRESS

CITY AND STATE   ZIP CODE

N1766--00002789

This appendix contains a sample of advertisements (many of which appeared in local newspapers and mass-mailed invitations) soliciting attendance at sales seminars. They are included as illustrative examples of the types of advertisements commonly used. Including them in this report does not indicate that they contain either accurate or inaccurate statements. The names of the sponsors, addresses, telephone numbers and other identifying information have been redacted.

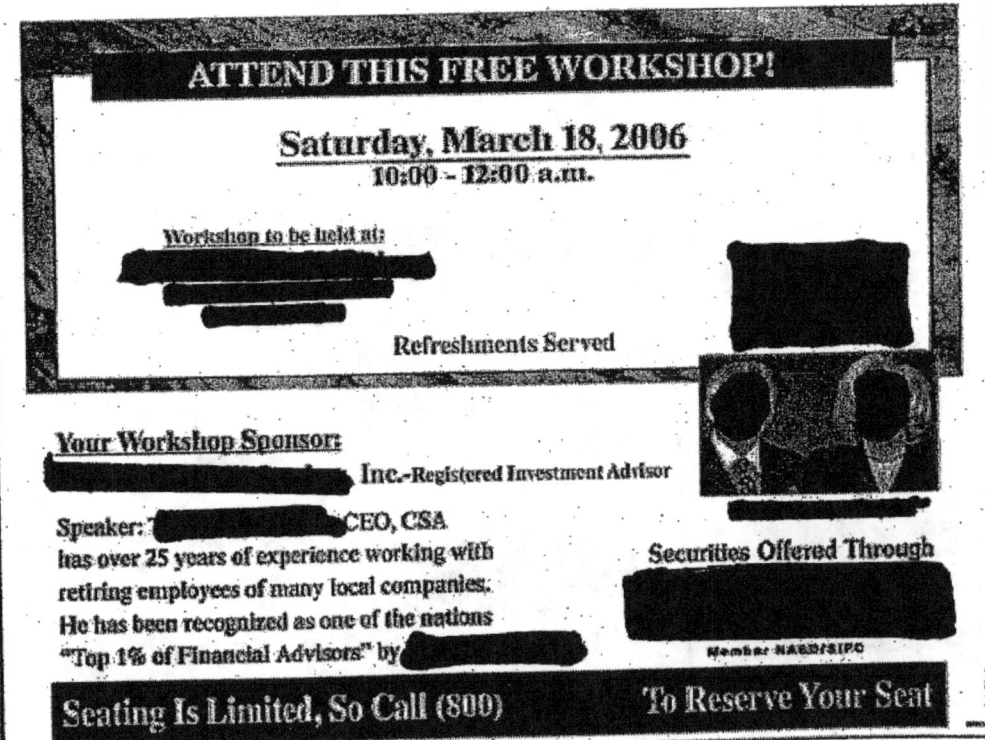

Is the Beneficiary of Your IRA the IRS?

Little Known Tax Laws Can Cost You Up to 71% Of Your IRA!

When Was The Last Time You Checked Your Beneficiary? Are You Sure You Have The Right One?

If You Are Retired Or About To Retire, Have Over $100,000 In IRAs, 401(K) and Other Retirement Accounts and Want To Help Protect Your "Nest Egg" From Being Taxed Up To **71%.**

Learn Strategies that can potentially help YOU:

* Reduce your required minimum distribution and **reduce your income taxes up to 42%** or more!

* Create a family legacy using tax-deferred compounding through an Inherited IRA Trust, which can last for 60 or more years.

* Determine who should and should not be the beneficiary of your IRA.

* Find out why leaving your 401(K) at your company after you retire may be a huge mistake.

* Take money out of your IRA tax-free through little-known strategies.

(Based on applying the highest Federal Income and State Income Tax rates at death as well as the highest Federal Estate Tax rate and IRS publication 915 regarding the taxation of Social Security Benefits) Please be sure to consult with a qualified tax advisor and an attorney.

ATTEND THIS FREE WORKSHOP!

Saturday, March 18, 2006
10:00 – 12:00 a.m.

Workshop to be held at:

Refreshments Served

Your Workshop Sponsor:

Inc.–Registered Investment Advisor

Speaker: ███████ CEO, CSA has over 25 years of experience working with retiring employees of many local companies. He has been recognized as one of the nations "Top 1% of Financial Advisors" by ███████

Securities Offered Through

Member NASD/SIPC

Seating Is Limited, So Call (800) ██████ To Reserve Your Seat

This appendix contains a sample of advertisements (many of which appeared in local newspapers and mass-mailed invitations) soliciting attendance at sales seminars. They are included as illustrative examples of the types of advertisements commonly used. Including them in this report does not indicate that they contain either accurate or inaccurate statements. The names of the sponsors, addresses, telephone numbers and other identifying information have been redacted.

This appendix contains a sample of advertisements (many of which appeared in local newspapers and mass-mailed invitations) soliciting attendance at sales seminars. They are included as illustrative examples of the types of advertisements commonly used. Including them in this report does not indicate that they contain either accurate or inaccurate statements. The names of the sponsors, addresses, telephone numbers and other identifying information have been redacted.

This appendix contains a sample of advertisements (many of which appeared in local newspapers and mass-mailed invitations) soliciting attendance at sales seminars. They are included as illustrative examples of the types of advertisements commonly used. Including them in this report does not indicate that they contain either accurate or inaccurate statements. The names of the sponsors, addresses, telephone numbers and other identifying information have been redacted.

APPENDIX B

EFFECTIVE COMPLIANCE and SUPERVISORY PRACTICES

During examinations of securities firms that provided "free lunch" sales seminars and in other examinations, examiners took note of several supervisory and compliance practices that appeared to be effective in ensuring adequate supervisory oversight and compliance with the securities laws with respect to sales seminars. These practices are described below. While these practices are not specifically mandated by the securities laws, individually or in combination they may be helpful to consider as securities firms are reviewing their supervisory and compliance practices in these areas.

Supervision of Seminars and Advertising

Regulators noted the following practices that were used in supervising individual registered representatives/investment advisers who held sales seminars and for reviewing and approving advertising materials for the seminars:

❖ The process for reviewing and approving proposed seminars and the advertising and other materials for the seminars was centralized, and included a dedicated compliance person with knowledge of the securities laws and rules with respect to advertising materials. The firm's policies and procedures clearly set forth the process for proposing seminars and advertising materials, and they were made known to all firm employees. Supervisory reviews of advertising and sales materials generally identified disclosure mistakes and potential problem areas that were corrected prior to the time the advertising materials were to be used.

❖ Policies and procedures for submitting proposals for sales seminars included specific timeframes for supervisory review and approval. For example, the approval and review process for seminar and advertising material required submissions of all materials three to four weeks prior to the seminar date. This allowed adequate time for supervisors to review and correct disclosure issues and any other issues identified prior to the seminar.

❖ All advertising material was forwarded to the home office for review and approval prior to use. This firm required information on seminar guest speakers to be forwarded and approved as well.

❖ One firm had two levels of supervisory approval for seminars and all sales materials and advertisements to be used at those seminars. The branch manager review was the first level of approval. The materials were then sent to the main office to be reviewed and approved by the compliance department.

❖ Written guidance was provided to all individuals who may be involved in sales seminars – the registered representatives who conduct sales seminars, the branch office manager and other supervisors who review and approve the seminars and sales materials as well as any compliance staff who may also review the sales seminars and materials prior to use. The guidance provided clear explanations of what was permissible and what was not permissible, both in terms of compliance with the securities laws, and compliance with the firm's own policies.

❖ Written checklists were used to aid firm employees in reviewing and approving sales seminar advertisements and sales literature to ensure that the materials used complied with regulatory requirements and the firm's policies.

❖ One firm's procedures required that supervisors or compliance staff make written edits to proposed sales seminar materials or advertising, and required that this marked-up draft be provided along with a final copy of the materials (showing that the changes had been made) to the reviewing official for the permanent file.

❖ Standardized, pre-approved materials and advertisements were used for sales seminars. The firm's procedures required that all marketing materials be created at a central level; individual registered representatives were not involved in creating their own seminar materials or advertisements. Registered representatives also used a standard outline for seminars.

❖ Materials for sales seminars were maintained in a centralized location. A complete package of seminar and advertising materials were filed and maintained in one place, including a copy of the request to host the seminar with indications of approval by the branch office manager and any other authorized approving official. The file included the title of the seminar, date, location, speaker, any guest speakers, the company they represent, the date the approval was given and the list of people who were invited to attend the seminar. The file also contained a list of attendees, whether they were a client or prospect, a photocopy of the actual seminar ad that ran in the newspaper, the approved marketing pieces that were distributed at the seminar, approved copies of the slide presentation and any other information given to attendees.

❖ Branch managers were expected to attend a percentage of the sales seminars presented by the sales people they supervised.

❖ "Mystery shoppers" (who were firm employees) were utilized on a random basis to attend sales seminars and to identify potential disclosure and compliance weaknesses, and report any issues back to the direct supervisors of the seminar hosts.

❖ All registered representatives were required to certify to their branch manager each month that they had provided all advertisements, sales literature, and correspondence items used during the month.

General Supervisory Practices

❖ Procedures explicitly addressed the review and monitoring of communications with clients and prospective clients. For example, monitoring systems were in place to effectively detect problematic communications by registered representatives in e-mail communications.

❖ The supervising principal actively reviewed correspondence, made frequent inquiries and provided feedback to the employed representative. This involvement appeared to enhance the firm's ability to identify and prevent any sales practice issues that may exist, and also provided supervised persons with individual training and guidance through active supervisory feedback on their communications.

❖ Annual training programs provided thorough and clear information about compliant and non-compliant practices. Training did not simply recite rule requirements, but included examples that were relevant to the nature of the work performed by the employees being trained.

APPENDIX C

RESOURCES FOR SENIORS

- The SEC provides important information for senior investors including explanations of different products, asset allocation and risk. You can also get information on affinity fraud, "senior specialists" and investment advisers and what to look for to identify and steer clear of potential frauds. http://www.sec.gov/investor/seniors.shtml

- FINRA also provides important information for senior investors. Its website has such items as *Broker Check* – that gives you the ability to look up the history of your investment professional to see if they have prior complaints or problems: http://www.finra.org/InvestorInformation/InvestorProtection/ChecktheBackgroun dofYourInvestmentProfessional/index.htm

  FINRA's website also has tools and resources to protect senior investors and help them make informed investment decisions, including "Investor Alerts" that provide timely information on steering clear of investment scams and problems instead of just dealing with their aftermath. Subjects of recent alerts include *"Look Before You Leave: Don't Be Misled by Early Retirement Investment Pitches That Promise Too Much," Annuities and Senior Citizens: Senior Citizens should be Aware of Deceptive Sales Practices when Purchasing Annuities," and "Seniors Beware: What you should know About Life Settlements."* http://www.finra.org/InvestorInformation/InvestorAlerts/index.htm

- The North American Securities Administrators Association (NASAA) also has helpful information available for seniors on its website: http://www.nasaa.org/Investor_Education/Senior_Investor_Resource_Center/

  Resources include: a quick checklist of questions to ask before you invest, 10 tips to protect your nest egg and guidance on where to turn for help.

- Regulators have warned that seniors may be confused by designations that imply some expertise in helping seniors. Information regarding professional designations is available through NASAA's Investor Alert is at www.nasaa.org, the SEC's information on professional designations at http://www.sec.gov/investor/pubs/senior-profdes.htm and NASD's professional designation database found at http://apps.finra.org/DataDirectory/1/prodesignations.aspx.